BEGINNER'S
SURVIVAL
COOKBOOK

Healthy dishes in 10 minutes!

D0752090

First edition: February 2012

Original title: *Recetas de supervivencia para principiantes*

© Lékué, 2011

© of this edition: Salsa Books, Grup Editorial 62, S.L.U., 2011, 2012

Peu de la Creu 4, 08001 Barcelona, Spain

correu@grup62.com

grup62.com

Recipes: Lara Canovas Garriga

Original idea and coordination: Lékué, www.lekuecooking.com

Nutritional information: Sticsa

Art direction and design: Nomon Design

Photo credits: Xavier Mendiola

Cook: Amanda Laporte

Translation: Discobole

Layout: Pau Santanach

Legal deposit: B-6330-2012

Printing: Creacions Gràfiques Canigó, sl

ISBN: 978-84-15193-11-1

BEGINNER'S
SURVIVAL
COOKBOOK

Healthy dishes in 10 minutes!

CONTENTS

Introduction

You don't know how to fry an egg. Or if you do, you're tired of eating the same old things every day. And, needless to say, you don't have time (or the will) to cook. If this is your case, then this is definitely the book for you! Here you'll find the necessary tools to get through your daily routine in an easy, balanced and tasty way: all you need is a microwave, a Lékué Steam Case and 10 minutes a day.

Surprise yourself with a delicious chicken risotto or curried loin of pork. Here we offer you a collection of **enjoyable, healthy recipes** made from ingredients within reach. They'll add variety and zest to your eating habits and do away with the monotony of your meals. Each recipe is very simple to prepare. By following each step, you'll create a perfect dish in next to no time.

To make things even easier, we've also included two **weekly menus** so that you don't have to rack your brains over what to cook for your next meal. These menus, designed by the Sticsa team of nutritionists, consist of nutritionally varied and balanced dishes to ensure that nothing is missing from your daily diet.

If you're one of those people who have a weekly date with a shopping trolley, be it a duty or a delight, save time by downloading the lists of all the ingredients you'll need for your weekly menus from **www.lekuecooking.com**.

With the aid of the tips and advice you'll find in this book, you won't have any excuse not to cook and eat healthy, balanced and appetising meals at home.

Cooking times for fresh food in the traditional oven and microwave

FOOD		QUANTITY	OVEN (400 °F / 200 °C)	MICROWAVE* (800 W)
VEGETABLES, RICE AND PASTA				
Artichokes	1/2 cup (100 ml) water, salt	2 units	15 min	7 min
Asparagus	1 tbsp water, salt	3/4 cup (150 g)	10-12 min	3-4 min
Aubergine		1/4 cup (60 g)	10 min	6 min
Broccoli and cauliflower	3 tbsp water, 1 tbsp olive oil, salt	3/4 cup (150 g)	15 min	4-5 min
Carrot	1 tbsp water, 2 tbsp olive oil, salt	1/4 cup (60 g)	15 min	7 min
Chard		1/4 cup (50 g)	10 min	3 min
Courgette	1 tbsp olive oil, salt	1/4 cup (60 g)	13 min	6 min
Leek	1 tbsp water, 1tbsp olive oil, salt	3/4 cup (150 g)	10 min	4-5 min
Mushrooms, fresh	1/2 cup (100 ml) water, 1 tbsp olive oil, salt	1/2 cup (100 g)	20 min	4 min
Onion	julienned, 1/2 cup (100 ml) water	1 cup (250 g)	12 min	4-5 min
Pasta, dried	1 1/2 cup (400 ml) water	1/4 cup (50 g)	30 min	10 min
Pasta, fresh	1 1/2 cup (400 ml) water	1/2 cup (80 g)	10 min	4 min
Pasta, stuffed	1 1/2 cup (400 ml) water	1/2 cup (100 g)	15 min	4 min
Pepper	2 tbsp olive oil, salt	1/2 cup (100 g)	12-15 min	4 min
Potato, medium size	diced, 3/4 cup (150 ml) water, 1 tbsp olive oil, salt	1 unit (60 g)	12 min	5 min
Rice	3/4 cups (200 ml) water	1/2 cup (80 g)	20 min	10 min
Runner beans	3 tbsp water, 1 tbsp olive oil, salt	1/2 cup (100 g)	12-13 min	7 min
Spinach	1/2 cup (100 ml) water, salt	3/4 cup (150 g)	10 min	3-4 min
Spring onions		1/2 cup (100 g)	10 min	4-5 min
Tomato	cut in half	1 unit	10 min	2 min
FRUIT				
Apple	cut into quarters, 1 tbsp water, 1 tbsp sugar	1 cup (200 g)	10-12 min	3 min
Banana	1 tbsp water	1 unit	12 min	1 min
Pear	cut into quarters, 1 tbsp water, 1 tbsp sugar	3/4 cup (150 g)	10-12 min	3 min
FISH				
Fish back (centre cut)		6 oz. (150 g)	10 min	3 min
Fish fillet	2 tbsp water	4 oz. (100 g)	8-9 min	2-3 min
Prawn tails	1 tbsp water	4 oz. (100 g)	10 min	2 min
SEAFOOD				
Clams and mussels	1/2 cup (100 ml) water	4 oz. (100 g)	10 min	2-3 min
MEAT				
Beef fillets		4 oz. (100 g)	7-8 min	2 min
Chicken legs		6 oz. (150 g)	7-8 min	2 min
Loin of pork	diced	6 oz. (150 g)	7-8 min	2 min
Rack of lamb		4 oz. (130 g)	12 min	2 min
Sausages		6 oz. (150 g)	7-8 min	3 min
Turkey breast	diced	6 oz. (150 g)	7-8 min	2-3 min
Egg	without the shell	1 unit	5 min	30 sec

* Times may vary depending on the power of the microwave used.

What is platinum silicone?

Platinum silicone is a type of silicone that only uses platinum (a noble metal) as a catalyst, thus making it totally odourless, antibacterial and **resistant to high and low temperatures.**

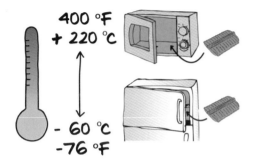

It is therefore perfect and absolutely safe for use in products such as surgical/healthcare materials, prosthesis, medical implants and **feeding bottle teats.**

Since it does not alter flavours or leave any residues, it is also ideal for manufacturing moulds and utensils that come into contact with food, as is the case for Lékué products.

In addition, its non-stick properties make **unmoulding easy.** As it does not need to be greased, it eliminates the overuse of butter and/or oil, thus offering a slightly healthier method of cooking, without any added fats.

For greater safety, Lékué applies strict quality controls and therefore guarantees a perfect end product. In addition to checking each and every one of the products, a post-curing process is applied, where the products are subjected to a temperature of 400 °F (215° C) for four hours to eliminate any possible residue. Consequently, you can **enjoy all of your meals with peace of mind.**

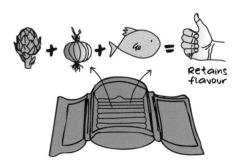

For a perfectly balanced day

If you organise your meals properly, it'll be easier for you to maintain a **stable weight** and ensure that your body gets the **energy** and **nutrients** it needs. You should try to eat four or five times a day and avoid going for long periods between meals.

Breakfast is the first and most essential meal. You'll have gone a long time without eating since dinner, so it is particularly important to start the day well.

Tip:
For it to be complete and balanced, breakfast should include three types of food: cereals, fruit and dairy products.

The main **meals** (lunch and dinner) should provide **complex carbohydrates** through food such as bread, rice, potatoes, pulses and pasta; proteins contained in meat, fish and eggs; and **vitamins, minerals, water** and **fibre** from vegetables.

Tip:
You should try to eat some raw plant-based food with each meal, such as salads, or fruit for dessert.

Tip:
One portion of vegetables is around 200 g, this is equivalent to a plate full

5 Daily portions

Tip:
A portion is equivalent to a glass of milk, two yogurts, a slice of mature cheese or an individual pot of curd cheese.

2
Daily portions

Food rich in complex carbohydrates

• Bread: daily consumption.

• Pulses (chickpeas, beans, lentils, soya beans): at least twice a week.

• Pasta: twice or three times a week.

• Rice: once or twice a week.

• Potatoes: four to six times a week.

Food rich in protein

• Red meat (ox, beef, lamb): once or twice a week.

• White meat (pork, chicken, rabbit, turkey): about three times a week.

• White fish and seafood (perch, monkfish, sole, scorpion fish, sea bass, red mullet, ray, halibut, turbot, cod, hake, plaice, prawns, mussels, cuttlefish, squid): three to four times a week.

• Oily fish (trout, salmon, sardines, skipjack tuna, herring, tuna, anchovies, mackerel, swordfish): at least twice a week.

• Eggs: about four eggs a week.

Dairy products

• Milk: daily consumption.

• Yogurt: daily consumption.

• Cheese: weekly consumption.

• Dairy-based desserts: occasional consumption.

Week one

If you organise your food well, you'll maintain an optimum state of health and also have more free time. To achieve that, plan your daily and weekly meals with the aid of the following menus.

	Day 01	Day 02	Day 03
BREAKFAST AND SNACKS	1 herb tea	1 bowl of cereals with milk	Tea with milk
	3 slices of toast with ham and curd cheese	1 pear	1 cured ham roll
	1/2 a papaya		1 glass of freshly-squeezed orange juice
LUNCH	Diced tomato with rocket	Chickpeas, red and green pepper, tomato and onion salad	Mixed-leaf salad with black olive vinaigrette
	Chicken and mushroom risotto with basil oil	Sea bass with courgettes and carrots	Curried loin of pork
	1 yogurt	1 apple	1 yogurt
TEA	1 drinkable yogurt	1 yogurt	1 drinkable yogurt
	2 tangerines	1 orange	3 figs
DINNER	Runner beans with potatoes	Endives with nut sauce	Broccoli with colored pasta spirals
	Hake in garlic and parsley sauce	Scrambled eggs with mushrooms on toast	Mustard plaice
	1 apple	1 drinkable yogurt	Fruits of the forest

Day 04	Day 05	Day 06	Day 07
1 herbal tea	Caffelatte	1 cup of hot chocolate with biscuits	1 glass of milk
3 slices of cheese on toast	1 turkey sandwich		6 biscuits
1 banana	1 apple	2 tangerines	1 mango
Cream of leek soup	Curly lettuce, cherry tomato and lentil salad	Mozzarella, tomato and basil salad	📋 Grated cauliflower with Emmental cheese
📋 Rice with beef strips	📋 Turkey breast with artichokes	📋 Rice with prawns	📋 Sausages with potatoes, onions and mustard
1 bunch of grapes		1 crème caramel	
	1 yogurt		1 pear
1 yogurt	1 yogurt	📋 1 portion of cheesecake with berries	1 yogurt
2 kiwis	2 tangerines		2 kiwis
Lettuce, tomato and beetroot salad	Cream of carrot soup	📋 Pesto macaroni	Sweetcorn and asparagus salad
📋 Potato frittata	📋 Layered vegetables	📋 Beefburger with caramelised onions	📋 Swordfish with baked apple and sweet-and-sour sauce
1 cuajada (a junket-style dessert)	📋 1 baked apple	1/4 a pineapple	1 kiwi

Week two

	Day 08	Day 09	Day 10
BREAKFAST AND SNACKS	1 herbal tea	1 bowl of cereals with milk	1 glass of milk
	3 slices of cheese on toast	2 tangerines	6 biscuits
	1 apple		2 kiwis
LUNCH	Lamb's lettuce salad	Cabbage and bean sprout salad	Tomato and mozzarella salad
	Pasta with dill salmon	Monkfish with mashed potato	Fresh seafood tagliatelle
	1 yogurt	1 drinkable yogurt	1 orange
TEA	1 yogurt	1 yogurt	1 drinkable yogurt
	1 orange	Grapes	1 banana
DINNER	Spinach with raisins and pine nuts	Pasta, curd cheese and pepper salad	Layered peppers, potatoes and grouper fish
	Country sausage with white beans	Courgette frittata	1 flavored yogurt
	1 pear	1 kiwi	

Day 11	Day 12	Day 13	Day 14
2 ham rolls	3 crackers with turkey	1 bowl of cereals with milk	1 caffelatte
1 yogurt	1 drinkable yogurt	1 orange	3 slices of toast with quince jelly
1 glass of freshly-squeezed orange juice	1 banana		1 glass of freshly-squeezed orange juice
Runner beans with cured ham	Mixed vegetables	Warm salad with frisée lettuce, tomato and salted cod	Mixed-leaf salad
Scrambled eggs with spring onions	Pork ribs with Teriyaki sauce	Fresh mushroom ravioli	Mussels with rice
Toast	1 apple	1 yogurt	1 drinkable yogurt
1 kiwi			
2 tangerines	1 yogurt	1 drinkable yogurt	1 yogurt
	2 kiwis	1 portion of apple or pear cake	1/4 a pineapple
Lettuce salad	Endive salad	Chard with chickpeas	Cream of pumpkin soup
Noodles with mushrooms and beef	Rice with tomato sauce and egg	Rack of lamb with herb dressing	Chicken legs with potatoes
1 yogurt	1 glass of milk	1 persimmon fruit	1 pear

How to buy for one person

Cooking for one doesn't mean that you can't eat healthily or enjoy a rich, varied diet. Below you'll find some simple pieces of advice that'll help you buy all the ingredients you need.

1

Buy loose fruit and vegetables. Irrespective of whether you shop at the supermarket or the greengrocers, the ideal thing to do is choose somewhere that allows you to by loose fruit and vegetables. This is the best option for a single person because it allows you to buy exactly what you need to help you get a varied diet.

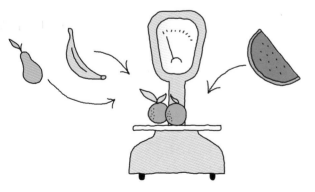

2

Stock up your cupboards. Many types of food already come prepared or canned. They are, therefore, a good option because they generally have very long expiry dates and keep well at room temperature. Always buy them in individual tins, jars, packets or cartons, and keep an assortment of them in your cupboards: tins of tuna, sardines, mackerel, cockles, clams, chopped tomato, asparagus, palm hearts, artichoke hearts, peppers, aubergines, olives, gherkins, onions, beetroot, carrots, mixed vegetables, soya sprouts, sweetcorn, pre-cooked pulses, dried vegetables for soups, etc.

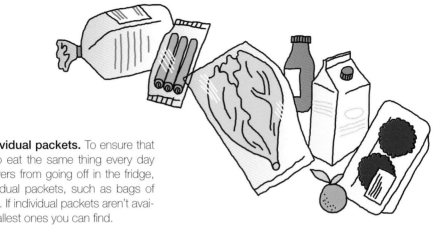

3

Buy food in individual packets. To ensure that you don't have to eat the same thing every day and to stop leftovers from going off in the fridge, buy food in individual packets, such as bags of lettuce or spinach. If individual packets aren't available, buy the smallest ones you can find.

4

Freeze individual portions. When buying fresh meat in trays, you can keep the portion you're going to eat soon in the fridge and put the rest in the freezer. Wrap each portion individually in cling film before freezing it down. By doing this, every day you'll be able to use only the amount you're going to eat. If any bread is leftover, you can cut it into slices and freeze it down. This means that you'll always have fresh bread available whenever you need it.

5

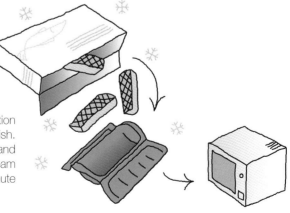

Opt for frozen food. Frozen food is a solution that'll allow you stock up with vegetables and fish. What's more, because they've been cleaned and cut up, you can cook them directly in the steam case without having to defrost them. Last minute improvisation is finally under control!

How to organize food items

To ensure that food stays fresh, it is very important to sort all items between your cupboards, your fridge and your freezer.

The place used as your cupboards should be cool, dry and dark. This is where you'll keep dry food: pasta, pulses, biscuits, rice, flour, tins, etc.

Tip:
Remember to store food items according to expiry date. When sorting them, put the ones with shortest expiry dates towards the front of the shelves.

Store perishable food that goes off more quickly either in the fridge or the freezer. The ideal temperature inside the fridge is 40 °F (between 4 and 5 °C) approximately. The temperature inside the freezer should always be kept at 1 °F (-18 °C).

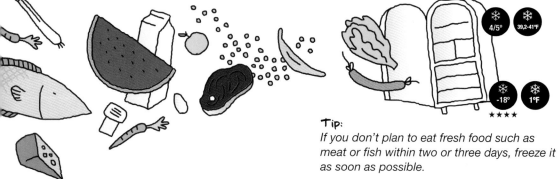

Tip:
If you don't plan to eat fresh food such as meat or fish within two or three days, freeze it as soon as possible.

In the fridge, place food items by group. Place meat and fish in the coldest part of the fridge, which is usually at the top; keep fruit, vegetables, dairy products and eggs in the least cold part.

Food should be well protected and identified. A ready meal, for example, can be kept in a covered plastic container with an Stretch Tops. If you open a packet of cold meat and have some left over, cover it with cling film.

Tip:

The amount of time that food can be kept in the fridge varies depending on the type, though it is never more than 30 days; in the freezer, however, it can be kept for up to 18 months.

If you decide to freeze food, divide it into individual portions and label them with the date. Freezer bags, such as Lékué Cooking Bags, are a very practical and airtight way of preserving food.

Defrosting

When defrosting food, you should always follow a number of food safety rules. Products should be defrosted in the fridge for approximately 24 hours before cooking them. Use a dish with a Defrosting Net on it so that liquids do not come into contact with the food.

If you ever need to defrost food quickly, you can do it in the microwave or even cook it directly from frozen by boiling it. Something you should never do is leave it at room temperature or bring it directly into contact with water.

Don't forget that defrosted food cannot be re-frozen unless it has been cooked. For example, if you've defrosted some minced meat and cook it with some macaroni, you can freeze the dish without any problem. But, you should remember that once cooked, it cannot be stored directly in the fridge or freezer until it has down. So you should leave it to cool at room temperature, but for no longer than two hours.

Note:

Despite all of these recommendations, you should carefully read the label of each product to ensure that you're storing it in the right place.

Week 01

Day 01

Chicken and mushroom risotto with basil oil

Runner beans with potatoes

Hake in garlic and parsley sauce

Day 02

Sea bass with courgettes and carrots

Scrambled eggs with mushrooms on toast

Day 03

Curried loin of pork

Broccoli with colored pasta spirals

Mustard plaice

Day 04

Rice with beef strips

Potato frittata

Day 05

Turkey breast with artichokes

Layered vegetables

Baked apple

Day 06

Rice with prawns

Cheesecake with berries

Pesto macaroni

Beefburger with caramelised onions

Day 07

Grated cauliflower with Emmental chees

Sausages with potatoes, onions and mustard

Swordfish with baked apple and sweet-and-sour sauce

Chicken and mushroom risotto with basil oil

Ingredients

1/4 cup (55 g) rice

2/3 cup (150 ml) water

2 oz (60 g) diced chicken

1 tsp (3 g) dried mushrooms

3 tbsp of olive oil

3 fresh basil leaves

1 tsp of grated Parmesan cheese

Salt

Pepper

Preparation

1 Put the rice, chicken, mushrooms, water and a pinch of salt and pepper in the Steam Case.

2 Close the case and cook in the microwave for 10 minutes at maximum power (800 W).

3 Remove the case from the microwave and dress with a little olive oil, chopped basil leaves and grated Parmesan. Mix well with a fork or spatula to bind together.

Runner beans with potatoes

Ingredients

- **1/2 cup** (100 g) runner beans
- **1** medium (60 g) potato
- **2/3 cup** (150 ml) water
- Salt
- Pepper

For the vinaigrette

- **1 tsp** of old-style mustard
- **3 tsp** of balsamic vinegar
- **6 tsp** of virgin olive oil

Preparation

1 Cut the runner beans and potatoes into small pieces. Put all the ingredients (except those for the vinaigrette) into the Steam Case. Close the case and cook in the microwave for 10 minutes at maximum power (800 W).

2 Remove the case from the microwave and make sure that the vegetables are cooked. If they are still a little hard, leave to rest in the case with the lids closed for 1 minute.

3 Mix all the ingredients for the vinaigrette together well and use it to dress the runner beans and potatoes.

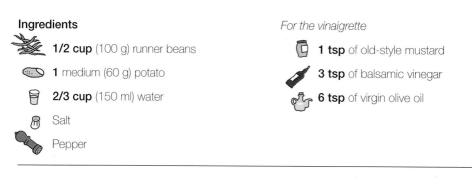

Tip:
You can also accompany this dish with a spoon-ful of mayonnaise and grated hard-boiled egg.

Hake in garlic and parsley sauce

Ingredients

 5 oz (150 g) hake (1 fillet)

2 tsp (10 ml) white wine

1 clove of garlic, chopped

Chopped parsley

Flour for coating

1 tbsp of olive oil

1/4 cup (60 ml) water

Preparation

❶ Season the hake with salt and pepper and coat it well in flour.

❷ Put the hake into the Steam Case with the rest of the ingredients.

❸ Close the case and cook in the microwave for 3 minutes at maximum power (800 W). Remove from the microwave and serve with the sauce.

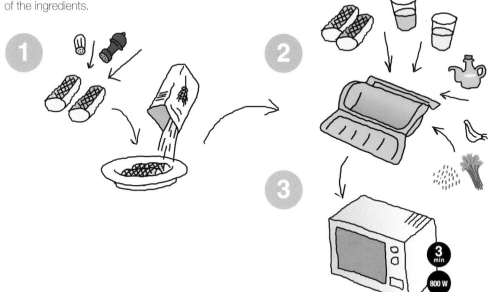

8 min   1

Sea bass with courgettes and carrots

Ingredients

1/4 cup (60 g) sliced carrots

1/4 cup (60 g) sliced courgettes

1 clove of garlic, chopped

1 1/2 tsp (6 ml) water

1 tsp of olive oil

3,75 oz (100 g) boneless sea bass (2 fillets)

1 tbsp of white vinegar

Chopped fresh coriander

Salt

Pepper

Preparation

1 Put the carrots, courgettes, garlic, water, oil, salt and pepper into the Steam Case. Close the Steam Case and cook in the microwave for 10 minutes at maximum power (800 W).

2 Season the sea bass with salt and pepper and put it among with the vinegar into the case. Close the lids and cook in the microwave for another 3 minutes.

3 Dress with chopped coriander and a few drops of olive oil.

Scrambled eggs with mushrooms on toast

Ingredients

1/2 cup (100 g) roughly chopped mushrooms

1/2 cup (100 ml) water

1 tbsp of olive oil

1 egg

2 tbsp (20 ml) milk

Salt

Pepper

Preparation

1 Put the mushrooms, water and olive oil into the Steam Case and season to taste. Close and cook in the microwave for 7 minutes at maximum power (800 W).

2 Beat the egg, milk and a pinch of salt and pepper. Remove the Steam Case from the microwave and fold in the beaten egg.

3 Close the lids and cook for another 30 seconds. Remove the case and gently stir the mixture. Close and cook for another 30 seconds. Serve on slices of toast.

Tip:
If you'd like to vary your scrambled eggs, follow the same procedure and replace the mushrooms with the same amount of spring onions or another type of vegetable. You can also accompany the dish with some julienned onion.

To find out about the cooking times for each type of vegetable, look them up in the cooking table.

Curried loin of pork

7 min   1

Ingredients

6 oz (150 g) loin of pork

1/2 cup (120 g) potatoes (1 medium potato)

1/2 cup (100 ml) water

1 tbsp of olive oil

1 sprig of fresh thyme

Curry to taste

Salt

Pepper

Worcerstershire sauce

Preparation

1 Dice the potatoes and loin of pork. Put the potatoes, water, oil, salt and pepper into the Steam Case. Close the case and cook in the microwave for 5 minutes at maximum power (800 W).

2 Add the loin of pork and season the dish with curry, thyme, salt and pepper. Mix well, close the lids and cook in the microwave for another 2 minutes.

3 Dress with a few drops of Worcerstershire sauce and serve.

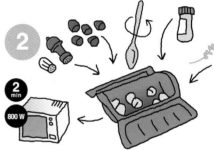

Broccoli with colored pasta spirals

Ingredients

1/4 cup (50 g) coloured pasta spirals

1/4 cup (50 g) broccoli

1 cup (250 ml) water

1 tbsp of olive oil

Oregano

For the vinaigrette

1 tbsp of soy sauce

2 tbsp of balsamic vinegar

1/3 cup (100 ml) virgin olive oil

Preparation

1 Put all the ingredients (except those for the vinaigrette) into the Steam Case. Close the Steam Case and cook in the microwave for 10 minutes at maximum power (800 W).

2 In a bowl, mix all the ingredients for the vinaigrette together well to form an emulsion.

3 Once the broccoli and pasta are cooked, dress with the vinaigrette and serve.

Mustard plaice

Ingredients

 6 oz (150 g) boneless plaice fillets

 1 tbsp of old-style mustard

4 drops of lemon juice

 1 tbsp of virgin olive oil

Salt

Pepper

Preparation

1 Put the plaice fillets in the Steam Case and season with salt, pepper, mustard and lemon juice.

2 Close the case and cook in the microwave for 2 minutes at maximum power (800 W).

3 Dress with olive oil and serve.

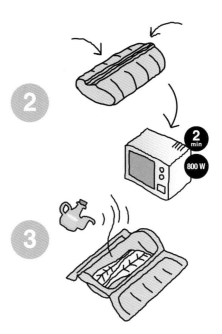

Rice with beef strips

Ingredients

1 cup of rice

3 cups of water

2 oz (40 g) beef, cut into strips

1 tsp of turmeric

1/8 cup (25 g) runner beans, cut into strips

1 tbsp of olive oil

Chives

Soy sauce

Salt

Pepper

Preparation

1 Cut the beef and runner beans into strips and chop the chives.

2 Put all the ingredients into the Steam Case and close the lids. Cook in the microwave for 10 minutes at maximum power (800 W).

3 Remove the case from the microwave and leave it to rest with the lids closed for 2 minutes. Then serve.

Potato frittata

Ingredients

1/2 cup (100 g) potatoes

1/4 cup (40 g) onions

2 tbsp of olive oil

1/4 cup (40 ml) water

2 eggs

Salt

Pepper

Preparation

1 Slice the potatoes fairly thickly and julienne the onions. Put the potatoes, onions, olive oil, water, salt and pepper into the Steam Case. Close the case and cook in the microwave for 7 minutes at maximum power (800 W).

2 Beat the egg and add it to the case. Mix well with a spatula or fork into the other ingredients.

3 Close the lids and cook in the microwave for another 2 minutes.

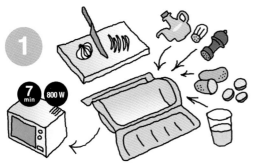

Tip:
If you'd like to vary your frittata, follow the same procedure and replace the potatoes with the same amount of courgettes or another type of vegetable. When using food with a high water content such as courgettes, reduce the amount of water to 20 ml.

To find out about the cooking times for each type of vegetable, look them up in the cooking table.

Week 01 Day 05

Turkey breast with artichokes

Ingredients

6 oz (150 g) turkey breast

2 artichokes

1/2 cup (100 ml) water

 Salt

Pepper

Worcerstershire sauce

Preparation

1 Clean the artichokes, cut them into quarters, season with salt and pepper and put the into the Steam Case with the water. Close the case and cook in the microwave for 7-8 minutes at maximum power (800 W)

2 Dice the turkey, season with salt and pepper and add it to the case along with the beer. Close the lids and cook for another 5 minutes.

3 Serve and dress with a few drops of Worcerstershire sauce.

Layered vegetables

15 min · 1

Ingredients

- **1/2** aubergine
- **1** medium potato
- **1/2** courgette
- **1 cup** (200 g) chopped tomato
- **1** tsp of sugar

- Grated cheese
- Salt
- Pepper
- Oregano

Preparation

1 Slice the vegetables thickly and season with salt and pepper. Add the sugar to the chopped tomato and mix well.

2 Place the vegetables in layers along with the chopped tomato into the Steam Case, alternating them. Cover with chopped tomato and grated cheese and then repeat the operation. Sprinkle a little oregano over the top and close the case. Cook in the microwave for 15 minutes at maximum power (800 W).

3 Make sure the vegetables are cooked, add extra salt if necessary and serve.

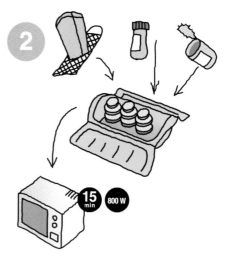

15 min · 800 W

Baked apple

Ingredients

1 Golden Delicious apple

1 tsp of sugar

1 tsp of butter

1 tbsp of water

Ground cinnamon

Preparation

1 Peel the apple, remove the pips and cut it into quarters.

2 Put all the ingredients into the Steam Case. Close and cook in the microwave for 3 minutes at maximum power (800 W).

3 Once the apple is cooked, remove the case from the microwave and leave it to rest for a few minutes before serving.

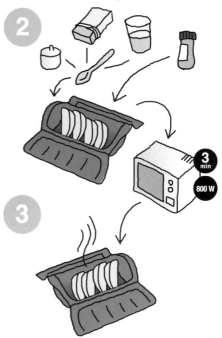

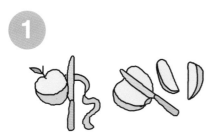

Tip:
If you feel like it, you can prepare this dish in advance and leave it to cool in the fridge for a delicious cold dessert.

Rice with prawns

12 min 1

Ingredients

1 cup of Thai jasmine rice	**1** clove of garlic
3 cups of water	**1** bay leaf
6 peeled prawn tails	**1** Chili pepper
1 cube of fish stock	Salt
1 tbsp of olive oil	Pepper
4 wild asparagus	

Preparation

1 Slice the asparagus lengthwise, leaving the tip whole.

2 Put all the ingredients into the Steam Case. Close and cook in the microwave for 10 minutes at maximum power (800 W).

3 Remove the case from the microwave and leave it to rest for 2 minutes. Then serve.

Cheesecake with berries

9 min

2

Ingredients

1 cup (250 g) cream cheese

6 tbsps of sugar

1/2 tbsp of corn flour

1 egg

Berries or blackcurrant jam

Preparation

1 Put all the ingredients (except the jam) into a bowl and beat until creamy.

2 Pour the mixture into the Steam Case. Close and cook in the microwave for 9 minutes at maximum power (800 W).

3 Leave it to cool before turning it out. Serve yourself a portion with some berries or blackcurrant jam.

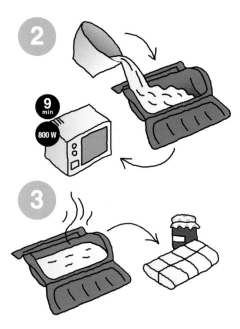

Pesto macaroni

Ingredients

1/2 tbsp (50 g) macaroni

1 cup (250 ml) water

Pesto sauce

Grated Parmesan cheese

Salt

Pepper

Preparation

1 Put the macaroni, water, salt and pepper into the Steam Case. Close and cook in the microwave for 10 minutes at maximum power (800 W).

2 Remove the case from the microwave and dress the macaroni with pesto sauce. Sprinkle some grated Parmesan cheese over the top.

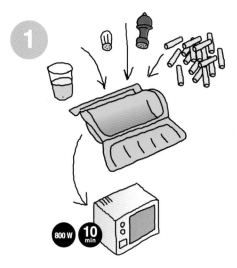

Tip:
For the pesto sauce, chop and mix one tablespoon of Parmesan, basil, pine nuts, 1 clove of garlic and 2 tablespoons of oil.

Beefburger with caramelised onions

Ingredients

- 🟤 **4 oz** (130 g) minced beef
- 🧅 **1 cup** (250 g) julienned onions
- 🥫 **1 tsp** of sugar
- 🥛 **1/2 cup** (100 ml) water

- 🫙 **1 tbsp** of olive oil
- 🍶 Worcerstershire sauce
- 🧂 Salt
- 🧂 Pepper

Preparation

Caramelised onions

1 Put the onions, sugar, salt, pepper and water into the Steam Case. Close and cook in the microwave for 15 minutes at maximum power (800 W), stirring occasionally and adding a little oil.

Beefburgers

2 In a bowl, mix the minced meat with Worcerstershire sauce, and knead well to ensure that the meat is fully infused with the flavours. Divide the meat into two balls and flatten them into beefburger shapes.

3 Add the beefburgers to the caramelised onions in the Steam Case. Close and cook in the microwave for 2 minutes 30 seconds at maximum power (800 W).

Grated cauliflower with Emmental cheese

Ingredients

3/4 cup (200 g) cauliflower

2/3 cup (150 ml) water

Grated Emmenthal cheese

Salt

Pepper

Preparation

1 Put the cauliflower, water, salt and pepper into the Steam Case. Close and cook in the microwave for 10 minutes at maximum power (800 W).

2 Add the grated Emmenthal cheese. With the case open, cook in the microwave for another 3 minutes to melt the cheese.

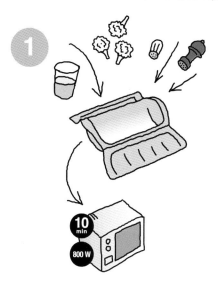

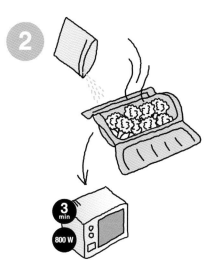

Sausages with potatoes, onions and mustard

Ingredients

3 sausages

3/4 cup (130 g) potatoes, cut into strips

1/8 cup (30 g) julienned onions

1/2 cup (100 ml) water

1 tbsp of olive oil

1 tsp of Dijon mustard

Sprig of rosemary

Salt

Pepper

Preparation

1 Cut the potatoes into strips and julienne the onions.

2 Put the potatoes, onions, rosemary, oil, water, salt and pepper into the Steam Case.

3 Close and cook in the microwave for 10 minutes at maximum power (800 W).

4 Add the sausages and the mustard and cook for another 3 minutes. Make sure the sausages are cooked and serve.

Swordfish with baked apple and sweet-and-sour sauce

Ingredients

5 oz (150 g) swordfish fillet

1 Golden apple

4 tbsp of white wine

1 tsp of butter

Lemon juice

1/4 cup (40 ml) water

Salt

Pepper

Rosemary

Thyme

Chives

Chopped parsley

Preparation

1 Chop the rosemary and thyme. Blend the herbs into the butter to form a smooth paste.

2 Peel the apple, remove the pips and cut into large dice. Dice the swordfish.

3 Season the apple and fish with salt and pepper. Put them into the Steam Case with the rest of the ingredients and spread the herb butter over the top. Close the case and cook in the microwave for 3 minutes at maximum power (800 W).

4 Sprinkle with chopped parsley and serve.

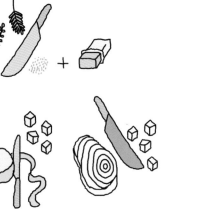

Week 02

Day 08

Pasta with dill salmon

Spinach with raisins and pine nuts

Day 09

Monkfish with mashed potato

Day 10

Fresh seafood tagliatelle

Layered peppers, potatoes and grouper fish

Day 11

Noodles with mushrooms and beef

Day 12

Mixed vegetables

Pork ribs with Teriyaki sauce

Rice with tomato sauce and egg

Day 13

Fresh mushroom ravioli

Apple or pear cake

Chard with chickpeas

Rack of lamb with herb dressing

Day 14

Mussels with rice

Chicken legs with potatoes

Pasta with dill salmon

11 min · 1

Ingredients

1/4 cup (50 g) penne

3,75 oz (100 g) fresh salmon

1 cup (250 ml) water

1 tbsp of olive oil

1 tsp of butter

Fresh dill

Salt

Pepper

Preparation

1 Put the penne, salt, pepper, oil and water into the Steam Case. Close and cook in the microwave for 10 minutes at maximum power (800 W).

2 Dice the salmon and chop the fresh dill. Add everything to the cooked penne with salt and pepper. Spread the butter over the top and close the case.

3 Cook in the microwave for another minute and then it will be ready to serve.

Spinach with raisins and pine nuts

Ingredients

1/2 cup (150 g) fresh spinach

1/2 cup (100 ml) water

1 tbsp (10 g) butter

1 tbsp of raisins

1 tbsp of pine nuts

Salt

Pepper

Preparation

1 Put the butter and pine nuts in the Steam Case. Close and cook in the microwave for 4 minutes at maximum power (800 W) to brown.

2 Put the rest of the ingredients in the case and close. Cook for another 5 minutes, stirring gently after 2 minutes.

3 Then it will be ready to serve.

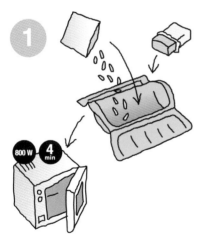

Monkfish with mashed potato

Ingredients

1 cup (200 g) sliced potatoes	
3/4 cup (180 ml) water	
5 oz (150 g) boneless monkfish (tail)	
1 bay leaf	
1 tbsp of olive oil	
Chopped parsley	

For the coating

Paprika

Thyme

Salt

Pepper

Preparation

1 Put the potatoes, water, salt and pepper into the Steam Case. Close and cook in the microwave for 15 minutes at maximum power (800 W).

2 Once cooked, mash the potatoes with a fork. Add the parsley and the oil, mix well and set aside in a bowl.

3 In the same steam case, coat the monkfish tail with paprika, salt, pepper and thyme. Once it is well coated, close the case and cook in the microwave for 5 minutes at maximum power (800 W).

4 Cut the monkfish into steaks and serve with the mashed potato.

Fresh seafood tagliatelle

4 min · 1

Ingredients

3 oz (80 g) fresh tagliatelle

1/2 cup (100 g) clams

1/2 cup (100 ml) water

2 tsp (10 ml) white wine

1 clove of garlic, chopped

1 tsp of chopped parsley

Oregano to taste

Salt

Pepper

Preparation

❶ Put all the ingredients into the Steam Case. Close and cook in the microwave for 4 minutes at maximum power (800 W).

❷ Dress with a few drops of olive oil.

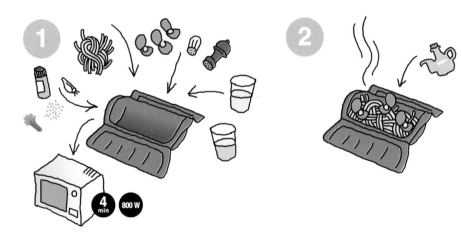

4 min · 800 W

Layered peppers, potatoes and grouper fish

Ingredients

- **1** red pepper
- **1** green pepper
- **2** small potatoes
- **3 oz** (80 g) boneless grouper fish (fillet)
- **3 tbsp** (40 ml) water

- Black olives
- Olive oil
- Salt
- Pepper

Preparation

1 Cut the red and green peppers in half lengthwise and slice the potatoes.

2 Put layers of the vegetables into the Steam Case, alternating slices of red pepper, potato and green pepper. Season with salt and pepper and add the oil and water. Close the case and cook in the microwave for 10 minutes at maximum power (800 W).

3 Add the grouper fish to the vegetables, close and cook for another 3 minutes.

4 Crush the olives to form a paste and spread it over the top of the grouper fish and the vegetables.

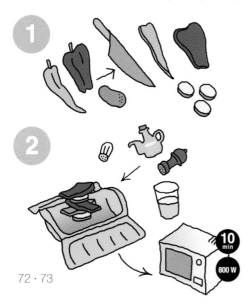

Noodles with mushrooms and beef

Ingredients

- **1/4 cup** (50 g) noodles
- **1/4 cup** (50 g) chopped mushrooms
- **1/4 cup** (50 g) minced beef
- **1 cup** (250 ml) water
- Chili oil*
- Salt
- Pepper

- Oregano

For the base

- **1** medium tomato
- **1** medium onion
- Olive oil
- Salt
- Pepper

Preparation

1 Finely chop the tomato and the onion together. Put the mixture, a few drops of oil, salt and pepper into the Steam Case. Close and cook in the microwave for 3 minutes at maximum power (800 W).

2 Finely chop the mushrooms and add them to the Steam Case with the rest of the ingredients. Close and cook in the microwave for 12 minutes at maximum power (800 W).

3 Stir gently and leave to rest for 5 minutes. Then it will be ready to serve!

Tip:
To make the chili oil, add a chopped chili pepper to a glass of olive oil and leave to infuse for at least 24 hours.*

Mixed vegetables

Ingredients

Baby carrots

1/2 cup (100 g) Runner beans

3 cauliflower florets

3 broccoli florets

1/2 diced potato

3 wild asparagus tips

1/2 cup (100 ml) water

Salt

Pepper

Preparation

1 Put all the ingredients into the Steam Case. Close and cook in the microwave for 4 minutes at maximum power (800 W).

2 Dress with chopped chives and thyme oil.

Pork ribs with Teriyaki sauce

Ingredients

 1 cup (260 g) pork rib, cut into pieces

1/2 cup (100 ml) white wine

Salt

 Pepper

For the Teriyaki sauce

2 tbsp of balsamic vinegar

6 tbsp of soy sauce

1 tbsp (15 g) sugar

Preparation

1 Season the pork rib pieces with salt and pepper and put them and the white wine into the Steam Case.

2 Close the case and cook in the microwave for 11 minutes at maximum power (800 W).

3 Add the Teriyaki sauce ingredients. Close the case and cook in the microwave for another minute. Mix well and serve.

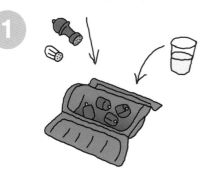

Cuban-style rice

15 min 40 s · 1

Ingredients

🍼 **1/4 cup** (55 g) short-grain rice

🥛 **1 cup** (250 ml) water

🥚 **1** egg

🧂 Salt

Pepper

🍌 Banana (optional)

For the base

🍅 **1** medium tomato

🧅 **1** medium onion

🫒 Olive oil

🧂 Salt

Pepper

Preparation

1 Finely chop the tomato and the onion together. Put the mixture with a few drops of oil, salt and pepper into the Steam Case. Close and cook in the microwave for 3 minutes at maximum power (800 W)

2 Put the rest of the ingredients (except the egg), including the banana if you feel like it, into the Steam Case. Close and cook in the microwave for 12 minutes at maximum power (800 W). Stir occasionally to make sure the rice cooks evenly.

3 Open the case and crack the egg over the top, taking care not to break the yolk. Season with salt and pepper, close the case and cook in the microwave for another 40 seconds.

4 Once the egg is cooked, it will be ready to serve.

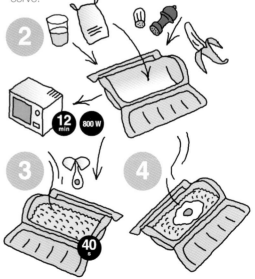

Fresh mushroom ravioli

4 min | 1

Ingredients

1/2 cup (100 g) fresh mushroom-stuffed ravioli

1/2 cup (100 ml) milk

1/2 cup (100 ml) single cream

1 tbsp grated Emmenthal cheese

Salt

Pepper

Nutmeg

Preparation

1 Put the milk, cream, salt, pepper and nutmeg mixture and the ravioli into the Steam Case. Close the case and cook in the microwave for 4 minutes at maximum power (800 W).

2 Once the ravioli are cooked, add a little Emmenthal cheese and leave to rest for 1 minute with the lids closed.

Apple or pear cake

2 min 30 s

2

Ingredients

3 tbsp (40 g) flour

3 tbsp (40 ml) olive oil

1/4 cup (50 g) sugar

1/2 tsp (6 g) baking powder

2 eggs

1 apple (or **1** pear)

Icing sugar

Preparation

1 In a bowl, mix all the ingredients (except the apple) together with a mixer.

2 Dice the apple and gently fold it into the mixture with a spatula.

3 Pour the mixture into the Steam Case. Close and cook in the microwave for 2 minutes 30 seconds at maximum power (800 W).

4 Make sure the cake is cooked by inserting a toothpick into it: if it comes out clean, it is ready; if it doesn't, cook it for another few seconds or leave it to rest with the lids closed.

5 Turn the cake out, sprinkle with icing sugar and serve.

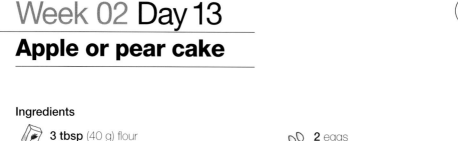

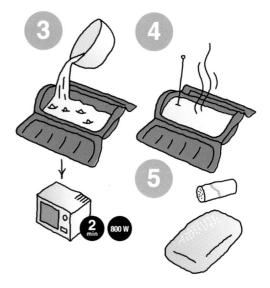

Chard with chickpeas

Ingredients

- **1/8 cup** (20 g) fresh, clean chard
- **3/4 cup** (150 g) chickpeas (ready cooked)
- **1 tbsp** of olive oil
- **1 tsp** of chopped toasted hazelnuts
- **1/2 cup** (110 ml) water
- Salt

- Pepper
- **1** medium tomato
- **1** medium onion
- Olive oil
- Salt
- Pepper

Preparation

1 Finely chop the tomato and the onion together. Put the mixture, a few drops of oil, salt and pepper into the Steam Case. Close and cook in the microwave for 3 minutes at maximum power (800 W).

2 Add the rest of the ingredients, close the case and cook in the microwave for 3 minutes at maximum power (800 W).

3 Remove the Steam Case and leave it to rest for 2 minutes before serving.

Rack of lamb with herb dressing

Ingredients

5 oz (130 g) rack of lamb
(prepared at the butcher's)

1 tomato, halved

1 tsp of water

For the dressing

1 tbsp of olive oil

Dry rosemary

Dry oregano

Dry parsley

Dry thyme

Salt

Pepper

Preparation

1 Mix the ingredients for the dressing and coat the rack of lamb with it.

2 Place the rack of lamb, the tomato cut in halves and the water into the Steam Case. Close and cook in the microwave for 2 minutes at maximum power (800 W).

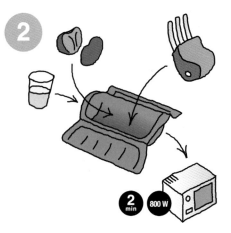

Mussels with rice

Ingredients

10 oz (300 g) mussels (preferably rock mussels)

1 tbsp (15 ml) white wine

Salt

Pepper

For the rice

1/4 cup (50 g) Thai jasmine rice

1 cup (190 ml) water

Salt

Pepper

For the base

1 medium tomato

1 medium onion

Olive oil

Salt

Pepper

Preparation

1 Finely chop the tomato and the onion together. Put the mixture, a few drops of oil, a pinch of salt and a pinch of pepper into the Steam Case. Close and cook in the microwave for 3 minutes at maximum power (800 W).

2 Add the mussels and white wine, close the case and cook in the microwave for another 2 minutes at maximum power (800 W).

3 Set aside the mussels in a dish. Add the rice, water, salt and pepper to the same case. Close and cook in the microwave for 10 minutes at maximum power (800 W).

4 Serve everything together and enjoy!

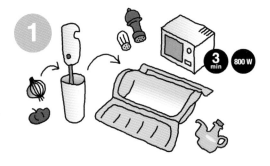

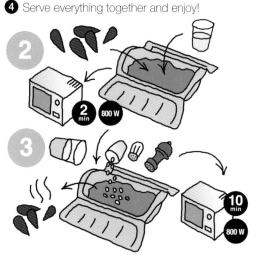

Chicken legs with potatoes

Ingredients

- **5 oz** (150 g) chicken legs
- **3/4 cup** (130 g) potatoes
- **1/8 cup** (30 g) onions
- **1/4 cup** (60 g) tomatoes
- **1 tbsp** of olive oil

- **1/3 cup** (80 ml) water
- **2 tbsp** (20 ml) white wine
- Thyme
- Salt
- Pepper

Preparation

1 Slice the potatoes and tomatoes and julienne the onions.

2 Put the potatoes, onions, tomatoes, white wine, water, oil, thyme, salt and pepper into the Steam Case. Season the chicken legs with salt and pepper and put them on top of the vegetables.

3 Close the case and cook in the microwave for 15 minutes at maximum power (800 W). Serve.